Sonnets to my Goddess

by

PHILIP HIGSON

FP
The Félibrige Press

© Copyright, 1983, by Philip John Willoughby-Higson
ISBN: 0 904448 15 0

Produced by:
The Bemrose Press/Cheshire Typesetters, 8 Canal Street, Chester
for the Félibrige Press
(an imprint of the Cestrian Press)
c/o Priestlands, Bunbury, nr. Tarporley,
Cheshire.

CONTENTS

Dedication — iv

Author's Preface — v

The Sonnets — 1

Notes to the Sonnets — 63

Index to First Lines of the Sonnets — 67

To M.H.H.

*"Rafael made a century of sonnets,
Made and wrote them in a certain volume
Dinted with the silver-pointed pencil
Else he only used to draw Madonnas . . ."*

– ROBERT BROWNING

*"These are the arks, the trophies I erect,
That fortify thy name against old age;
And these thy sacred virtues must protect
Against the dark, and Time's consuming rage."*

–SAMUEL DANIEL

Author's Preface

This century has excelled in nothing so much as the severance of cultural continuities, and has bred many perverse and arrogant myopes who exult in that severance and worship meretricious novelty. The present collection is the work of one who, on the other hand, cherishes the former centuries of European civilization and believes (rather quaintly, some will think) that one of the best ways of honouring an evolving and deepening love-relationship is a sequence of sonnets. When the right circumstances arose I found myself quite naturally building on the literary tradition established by Petrarch in the early Renaissance, a tradition founded in its turn on the lyrical precedent of the troubadours, whose influence contributed to the discovery of the sonnet form in 13th-century Sicily. I had become quite accustomed to writing in that form among others by the time the relationship blossomed which is portrayed in the present sequence, and without the least premeditation I at once began to express and acclaim that relationship in a variety of sonnets — Sicilian, Petrarchan, Shakespearean, etc.

I would emphasize that it was living love that carried me along as I did so, not some desire to execute an antiquarian intellectual exercise. Indeed, at some points, empirical reality outstripped my knowledge of literary history. For example, my beloved and I were confronted by a perfect real-life example of the 'losengier' (a scandal-mongering saboteur of love) long before we knew that the troubadours, like the Arab poets who influenced them, had complained repeatedly of that most odious of creatures. I confess that, as one who values cultural continuity, I was gratified to find that I had been continuing here a literary theme traceable, through the Moors of Spain, at least as far back as ninth-century Baghdad! But it was not intended that way. Indeed, I would rather the 'losengier' had never made his appearance in real life to inflict his tortures and to have his literary portrait drawn by my pen, but so radiant and conspicuous is love that it rarely escapes the attentions of his (or her) malevolent envy.

But I do not wish to deter my reader by mentioning only the darker tones of what is essentially a chiaroscuro canvas. This is a story of the ultimate triumph of human love over all adversity. The radiance of human love, without which life is a mere shadow and religion itself a cold and cruel travesty, has been reverently portrayed here in many of its innumerable glittering facets. Human love is the hero of this lyrical narrative, giving battle not only against the 'losengier' but against other enemies too, like enforced separation, deadening routine, overwork and illness, or the puritanism of the Hebraic tradition. In its triumphant conclusion it reflects my conviction that the battle to preserve a noble love within this life, and not relegated to some realm of metaphysical abstractity, is infinitely worthwhile and is what in the end distinguishes a man from a mouse! I remain, however, a troubadour to the last, for the supreme purpose of this sequence is to pay due homage to the rarest of women, without whose understanding and compassion and charity there would have been no triumph at all.

P.J.W-H.

Chester,
September, 1983.

Acknowledgements

The majority of the sonnets printed here have already appeared in annual anthologies of work by the Chester Poets, and I am indebted to the group as a whole and to its editorial committees for much sensitive appraisal and encouragement. But (again it must be said) without the inestimable contribution of a most remarkable woman, without her many distinguished qualities and beauties, there would quite simply have been nothing for me to celebrate, and no love-poetry in existence to publish.

I

An evening bathed in gold, pale Grecian light;
A lecture's pictures rich upon a screen,
A voice of bronze that spoke in accents keen
Of Art's Renaissance from medieval night.

Italian names that chimed for our delight;
Grew soft like 'Raphael' at his forms serene,
Roused with 'Giorgione' to a warmer scene
Then 'Titianed', 'Tintorettoed' out of sight.

For here the story gained its blissful end,
Havened in bland Venetian harmony;
But still I marvelled, for my spellbound gaze

Had found you, living, yet in radiant blend
With those bright visions of antiquity —
You, whom my heart, no less than eyes, would praise.

II

I dwelt alone in dreams, and if my dream —
Though years before we met — resembled thee,
And words addressed in wistful reverie
To melting phantoms now familiar seem,

Pray do not blame that early quest, nor deem
As wantons my poor hands that haplessly
Pursued your mirage through vacuity —
They did but dabble in an aery stream.

Sometimes in that far nightmare shone a line
Fit for the portrait known today as thine,
And pulse and pen would race until it paled;

But poor the deeds of my deluded Muse
Till by the sole true source at last regaled
I paint at ease all love's and beauty's hues.

III

With heart, with soul, with wit, with will,
With looks, with lips, with limbs, with loins,
With all that love with love conjoins,
With every ardour, every skill,

I shall thee worship and thee serve,
I shall thee praise and thee exalt,
And banish from me stain and fault
That would impair our tender verve.

I shall acclaim in thee my shrine,
In thee my model and my Muse,
And from thy palate sip the wine
That gilds my life with richer hues,

But, oh, the rapture when, unplanned,
To prove us plighted, hand meets hand.

IV

To thank all Gods, to tell all men
My joy in thee, and in me thine,
Let, monstrance-wise, our true love shine
And bear new hope into their ken;

Let us be as an altar when,
By mystic rite of bread and wine,
The timeless essences divine
Reclaim their earthly regimen;

Let us in union deep as heaven,
And close-knit as the sky's own hues,
To famished mortals not refuse
Our rich largesse, our potent leaven;

Nor stint in praise those nameless powers
Who planned the bounty that is ours.

V

I love your being like my mother, Earth,
And father, Heaven — yes, and more than these.
In your appraisal is my test of worth,
Without your happiness I have no ease.

I love your fond heart and your friendly hand,
I love your chatter rippling through the air,
I love your mirth when I'm absurdly grand
Or your soft whisper soothing my despair.

I love your candour though it bring me pain,
I love the artless girl who lingers still,
Or the rare woman, scorning to be vain.

With every plunge, to some new pearl I thrill,
And yet you brand me with the dark disgrace
Of loving but the shallows of your face!

VI

What shallow strangers were we at the start;
What flippant words to flippant words addressed;
With supple foil we bantered with the best,
And did not dream that Cupid poised his dart.

And now your hands, your lips are on my heart,
And now my tears forgather at your breast,
And now each thought is by its kin caressed
That, to one sweetness, sweeter will impart.

I have no being, now, except in you,
Nor is there world, unless from us it spring;
Without our sun to bid them thrive anew

There are no flowers, there is no harvesting;
And now, in all I plan and all I do,
I tend a gift . . . that is the gift you bring.

VII

At love's first coming we were both new-born,
Our eyes all wonder at the pristine day;
Life was a torrent, volatile and gay,
That sparkled in the robes of golden dawn.

And were we wrong, about that radiant morn
To run like children drunken at their play,
To shun the solemn and the ordered way
And swim the perfumed waves of breast-high corn?

It was no crime, but I to love you now
Must face a changeful world with dauntless prow,
And in my vessel fold your tender form
Like a pale fledgling in a kindly palm,

That, through the menace of each mouthing storm,
Your heart may know my cradle, and be calm.

VIII

Love at its birth is like the 'given line'
That starts a poem on its fair career,
A motion in the heart, a sudden cheer
That comes unsought when heaven is benign.

And none can simulate its breath divine
Or sail without it o'er the briny sphere,
But none can either, though it hover near,
Upon that presence mindlessly recline.

We needs must trim the canvas, tend the helm
Lest that which blessed us first should overwhelm
And plunge our vessel in the gulf despair.

Nor name it false, this labour of the brain
To rescue from the wrack affection's care:
The breeze, the mariner, we need these twain.

IX

Our life in miniature: you, lithely poised —
A very Cleopatra — in the stern;
I, striking at the tide, our forefoot noised
By my rude vigour that you deftly turn.

I gaze upon your loveliness, and heave
To say I am a man, and would deserve
(If merit can) your plaudits to receive;
You mark the distance with unwavering nerve.

I am all vehemence, and will, and strife
While you ride close and laugh away my frown;
Your heart is given, my betrothed, my wife,
Yet I would earn it still with new renown:

I hope that you (in secret) watch my oars
And would be hurt if basely they should pause.

X

Be thou my friend and of all friends my best,
Be thou my sister of the same proud line,
Be thou my child and nestle to my breast,
Be thou my mother, taking me to thine.

Be thou the guardian angel of my heart,
Be thou the altar where my soul may kneel,
Be thou the model worshipped of mine art,
Be thou the Muse and Goddess of my zeal.

Be thou my priestess in love's glorious rite,
Be thou my playmate and my bedfellow,
Be thou my bubbling spring of pure delight,
Be thou my kindling spur when wit is slow.

Be thou mine ally in the war of life,
Be thou mine all of these . . . and be my wife.

XI

The greatest loves with sharpest fears must dwell:
With fears of less than permanence or truth,
With fears that joy may break on reefs of ruth,
With fears a miraged heaven may veil new hell;

So we both tremble for the fragile spell
We weave between us in the dew-bright youth
Of our denuding day, and fear the drouth
In full meridian's gaze, perverse and fell.

But let us make this pact, that out of night
Our hearts together walk in perfect plight
To more, and more; and whisper at my side
Three words — 'I trust thee' — in one reckless breath.

Then this poor human breast shall burst with pride
And keep such faith that it shall outwill death.

XII

When you revealed your faith to be so frail
In that rare soul my being most reveres,
Explaining your enormity of fears
As though of this disease I could not ail,

My poor heart smiled to see the semblance pale
Of its own vivid terrors and gross tears,
Of those dark hours when all creation jeers
And utters the damnation: you will fail!

Strange irony, that you should seek to tell,
For understanding, what I know so well
And maybe better! Should it not be I
Confessing unto you my gloom's abyss

That, when I blench and grieve, you too know why
And we may quench twin horrors in one kiss?

XIII

I cannot speak your creed and yet I stand
Turned altarwards with you at evensong,
For where you are, there also I belong
By no less patent than our love's command.

If yours the kindly God who brought us near
Or made your heart so fond and you so fair,
Then I would have Him in our rapture share
And bless my human love that holds you dear.

Then I would offer Him like you, sweet shrine,
The thanks and homage due to the divine
As now I do, although these lips be dumb
While heavenwards the fitting words are poured.

But load me not with dark opprobrium:
Little you hear when *you* are most adored!

XIV

I am a pagan of the Grecian strain
Who must be whole in flesh and heart and mind,
Yet sometimes fail and, after failing, find
That you, like Christ, redeem me with your pain.

I am a pagan who abhors the stain
By slanderous Jewry spattered on Mankind,
I shall not kneel among the castrate blind
Who worship loss where God has all the gain.

I am a pagan and patrician proud
Who by no vulgar credo shall be cowed,
But vaunt his honour above all the jeers
Of those who swarm in bloody Dogma's train.

I am a pagan, yet I say through tears
That you, like Christ, redeem me with your pain.

XV

I could not love thee more, yet shall love more;
I have thy love, yet every day would woo
That heart, of all most ardent and most true,
Offering its tender need my proofs most sure:

If tears are sought, then tears as warm and pure
As our dear flame shall for thy favour sue;
If sacrifice and hazard best renew
My quest of thy sweet hand, give me full store.

Let waking hours bring all the cares they will
If they but strengthen what they strive to kill:
Taunt us like furies if they flee like churls
And we can wed at dusk who blenched at noon;

Then, as the blue flower of our night unfurls,
Can breathe smooth balms of new-found honeymoon.

XVI

How hard it is to keep one's loftiest aim
Amid the spate of small quotidian things:
One bursts one's heart yet cannot spread one's wings;
One reels and falters, in despair of fame.

I bore myself, I bow myself with shame
At the dull humour repetition brings;
And, writhing limply in the net that clings,
I tremble lest to you I look the same . . .

Until I hear your voice describing too,
With the rich timbre that I know so well,
The trivia that the day has forced on you

And find how undiminished is your spell,
Your peerless skill to summon up anew
The will and mettle of your Astrophel.

XVII

When a rare heart draws close to me as yours
And shares its utmost tenderness and sweetness,
Wreathes from the day-drudge dross my soul abhors
A rival world of splendour, joy and meetness,

And though made blissful in this new dimension
I blink and stumble still with long confinement,
My vision blurred, my powers in mute suspension,
Suffering and bringing pain of cruel refinement,

When I contrive to torture where I cherish
And nonetheless am readily forgiven,
Then I would weep till time and conscience perish
At the fond breast that is my bounteous heaven,

Then I would kiss in every glorious part
The one I'd hurt, and calm that peerless heart.

XVIII

The book our love is writing with one pen,
Held by your hand and mine alternately,
Is like a spreading realm where vale and tree
And lake and mountain glide into our ken;

Sweet thoughts and blissful moments, breathed again,
Assuage the wounds of life's enormity,
And spacious aisles of deathless memory
Renew our joy despite the world of men.

Our paradise expands with every day
That we can claim as ours who hold at bay
The pigmy-trivial and the foul-profane;

Love is a searching for the pristine spring,
The sheltering foliage, in a parching plain,
And broad leaves flourish where our teardrops cling.

XIX

The measure of your love amazes me —
I, who so vaunt in verse my aureole flame
That, never wavering, gilds effulgently
Your moment's beauty with a Muse's fame,

Owe all to you, am by your heart outshone
As moonless midnight is by cloudless noon,
Blessing most meek, though equal you have none,
Who find such joy in bearing me your boon.

My boasted radiance falters in affright
At fancied phantoms, and at once your hand
Is near to calm that fever-haunted light;

Injured yourself, you search and understand
The pain I curse in, and with suavest cures
You brace my heart that it may partner yours.

XX

Reft of the presence that my heart most craves
I dream you near me through the dragging days,
I count like holy beads your varied ways
And swim remembered love's assuaging waves.

I walk with you again through stately naves,
With you again my spirit bows and prays,
With you I comb the heavens with grateful gaze
And thank the power that gives, the power that saves.

I reach towards our Eden's flown content,
Call to those peerless hours, so swiftly spent,
And plead aloud with bliss's plunderer;

But time that took you from me will not halt
And time that must return you will not stir,
And life without you is an echoing vault.

XXI

Distance shall not untune the pulse of love
Nor mute the passing of a dear-held day,
My heart's clear chime, an earth, a death away
Would to this challenge more than equal prove.

Withheld from you, while knowing that my dove
Is butchered by coarse hands I cannot stay,
This breast is like some torture's hapless prey
By gag and bond forbade to speak or move.

But our day comes, and some means shall convey
This beat of light although the clouds hang grey
And blot from sight the succouring arm above;

These lines announce our love's unfaltering sway
And beg you, my true home, to spurn dismay
And through dark winter dream of our green grove.

XXII

When you are low, my love, remember this:
That there is one whose idol you remain,
Who hopes, and prays his hopes will not be vain,
To know again your blessing and your bliss;

That there is one who, though he cannot kiss,
Still yearns to reach you with his soul's refrain,
And from his distant exile ease your pain
By setting right what fate contrives amiss.

And, for that one, the only one is you:
The only Muse his genius answers to,
The only woman on this giddying sphere

Whom he would ply each night through every pore
With paeans of devotion and good cheer.
Remember this, rare heart, and grieve no more.

XXIII

Like a parched landscape calling out for rain
My lonely body burns and yearns for yours;
When from afar you speak, my spirit soars
But my loins pine with even fiercer pain.

I lie down grieving like some withered plain
And curse my dearth and distance without pause,
While over night's bleak void my fancy draws
A mirage of your beauty's shimmering train.

When will your gentle mercies fall and feel
My brooding contours? When will lips and hands
And potent breasts like laden gourds assuage?

When will you open heaven and softly seal
Its concord with my madly thirsting sands,
And in their arid bed make torrents rage?

XXIV

When we have made of night the calm terrain
Wherein we lie with nudity our friend,
Our bodies and our hearts at will to blend
And in uncounted ways form one of twain,

When we have swum entwined a single main
Where limbs and dreams and tears and kisses wend,
When we have found how tenderness can mend
And how by reckless gift of love we gain,

Then let the world and daytime do their worst
Where with the rest we grind through roles rehearsed
To gratify the groundlings of an hour,

For in that haven with our blessings filled
Dark memories shall blench at passion's power
And by fond solace shall the soul be stilled.

XXV

Gleaming new-minted on our pristine night,
With arms upflung, brave breasts and laughing lips,
Meandering waist, suave midriff, rapturous hips,
Your whole form radiant after love's glad rite,

You bathed my dizzied gaze in lustred light
From blissful brow to tendril fingertips
To seashell toes, moon-clear of all eclipse
And revelling as I reeled at stunned first sight!

Before that dazzling brilliancy I bowed
And kissed your soft oasis, warm and proud,
Where, minutes past, my blood had poured its tide;

And then I rose, to eyes where fond fires glowed,
To ripe lips yearning, and to arms thrown wide
That bade my heart reclaim its heart-abode.

XXVI

Your rapture breathes still at my pillowed ear,
Still of your limbs these silks are redolent
And hoard the treasures of your musk unspent
That my lungs drain, still dreaming you are near.

This day, my Dearest, wrought you far more dear,
And brought that boon of uttermost content
When hearts true-plighted have their bodies blent
In first communion, conquering all fear.

And still you touch me where your hands grew bold,
And still your fretful trust, at length consoled,
Imparts its presence, beautiful and grave;

Our bed, where kissed lips could all secrets tell,
Echoes with soft responses like a nave:
The shrine is hallowed, where our love shall dwell.

XXVII

My lips have scarcely yet begun to pay
That homage which they owe your loveliness —
They who would kiss your all, from sable tress
To golden instep, in stupendous play;

They who, to find your coyest pore, would stray
Companioned by my clairvoyant caress
About your blushful body's tenderness,
Taunting you always in some new-found way.

But should you dream of any jewel of bliss
I fail to bring you, let your ruse be this:
Take my forefinger in your dexterous hand
And bear it to that place I fail to please;

And there, in honour of this mute command,
My love shall craze you with its gallantries!

XXVIII

In some soft place — you have not told me where —
You love the kiss of eyelash-butterflies:
Deft half-confession that will tantalize
And spur my quest until I craze you there!

First to your throat and nape shall fluttering fare
My fragile wings' caress, and then surprise
The nook that by your amber shoulder lies,
And then those breasts where ardour waits to flare,

Then wrists, then palms of hands or palms of feet,
Then crook of knee, suave midriff, navel neat,
Smooth inner thigh or inward slope of hip
That draws me to your fronded Venus-mound.

Should you be blissless yet, my swarm shall dip
To claim your nectared womb, its haven found!

XXIX

Let those drab souls devoid of comely parts
Deride sweet love and lock themselves away
In some plain chapel where they prate and pray
Against the horrors wrought by Cupid's darts;

Let those who will not learn the beauteous arts,
The gentleness, the worship, and the play
Whereby we make our human partners gay,
Bar from the sun their breasts that have no hearts;

Let all ill-favoured misers hide their shame
In cloth and cloister so that no man knows
The nightmare of their natures, warped and lame;

While you, so fond, so fair, your all disclose
That lines like these may earn you rightful fame
And to my warm lips I may raise your rose!

XXX

Echoing with glory still but fallen low,
In the plebeian deluge islanded,
My brooding house, now paralysed with dread,
Shunned the fine gestures of its former show.

Forever fearful of some crueller blow,
It closed its doors on life, and I was fed
A sullen, proud and rigid creed instead
And all the dark dearths of Malvolio.

Taught to mistrust both mind and comely form,
The artist festered and the lover soured;
I fought to break my fetters, and a storm
Of maledictions lashed me where I cowered;

My heart was petrified and would not warm
Until you shone on me . . . and worship flowered.

XXXI

You are my blessing, and I bless your name.
In you I found my home, I found my kin;
All things around you, all my heart within,
You gild with beauty like a solemn flame.

With who knows what celestial guide you came
Bearing your warmth to mine, its waiting twin;
Trusting and offering most, the most to win,
And in one radiance two devotions frame.

And now no altar that the creeds revere
Holds truer prayers than yours when I adore
That hallowed form with kiss, caress and tear.

My soul has whispered through your every pore
Its whole sweet essence for your love to hear
And grow of mine as sure as I am sure.

XXXII

Your person is my world, my fair demesne:
Your flesh my pasture, hair my foliage;
Your eyes are tranquil pools that calm life's rage,
Your voice's murmur soothes a summer scene;

Your mouth's a grotto past whose crystal sheen
Cool rillets glide from some still taintless age;
Your breasts are Eden fruits at ripened stage
Whose tender spheres look sunward as they lean;

Your loins are massy dunes where sink my hands
And neath dense fronds your suave oasis hides;
From pole to pole my love's proud huntsman rides
The softly-contoured limbs that bound your lands;

Your feet are like white doves, both swift and shy,
Whom I shall chase, then kiss until they die!

XXXIII

What firmer proof than this be there of love? —
Than all night long another's pain to tend;
Pain of a stranger, hard to comprehend,
But known in need, and this enough to move.

My Dearest, you have loved, with love that throve
Through all my darkness, selflessly to blend
Your honey with my gall, your goal to mend
My grief, your fair form cleaving like my glove.

O humbling heaven, to feel you change your pose
With every motion that my slumber chose
Intent through all my torment to console;

To feel your perfect breasts and loins and limbs
Knead themselves to me in a healing shoal,
This was to learn your praise with timeless hymns.

XXXIV

I thought that I had long since learnt to care,
I thought my heart was plighted to your cause,
I thought that your betrothed was truly yours
Until that night you wooed me from despair.

My blundering love had trod some ancient snare
That held me from you with its rending jaws,
But you released and kissed my wincing sores
And found it sweet my bitter fate to share.

Till hopeful dawn, pretending sleep, you chose
To follow me through every fitful pose
With ministering lips and soothing breast
And close embrace that like a garland twined.

You wept, in silence, lest you marred my rest;
And taught me all, who was till then stone blind.

XXXV

To wake as those first veils fell from the sky
And Dawn's proud chorus-master poised his hand,
To lap myself in limbs that understand
And slake my heart with love too deep to die;

To watch your beauty growing with the light,
To meet your eyes and touch your lips and smile,
To know that in our Eden dwells no guile,
That soul and body are in flawless plight;

To mark how gentle word and soft caress
Had merged within a mystic blessedness
Which made us one and radiant as the sun:

This was to feel my frail hope rise anew —
All praise to some rare Deity, and you —
Rise burnished clean of days less well begun.

XXXVI

Your eyes, so dark they pale the deepest night,
Are yet so lustrous that they dim the sun,
Are jewels rare that fill my heart with light,
Are velvet wells of bland oblivion.

Within them glints my own clear firmament
That guides my moods more surely than the stars,
And when in one sweet gaze our hearts are blent
They melt away life's pain and smoothe its scars.

The world grows powerless when I feel their rays
And vain portentous Man becomes a clown,
Envy falls dumb at verse's potent praise
And habit's manacles drift off like down.

Your eyes shine on. My worship shines reply,
And heaven is here, and passing angels sigh!

The Envious Angels

Let me tell you about the envious angels:
Those who divide their time
Between ostentatiously polishing their haloes,
And slyly peeping round deceptively innocent clouds
Wreaking anonymous sabotage.

Let me tell you of the pale who envy health
And the sterile who envy fecundity
And the ugly who envy loveliness
And the unlovable who envy love.

Let me tell you of the crazed who envy reason
And the inert who envy attainment
And the insensitive who envy perception
And the gross who hate what's fine.

Let me tell you of the craven who envy courage
And the feckless who envy pride
And the prostitute who envy honour
And the slime that envies fire.

Let me warn you to be on your guard
Against the envious angels:
Whether they take the form of the holy
And of another world,
Or whether their obsession is to mix
A cold grey gruel of equality in this
(In which, by the way, my friend
You'd be quite invisible).

Behind the so plausibly altruistic
And altitudinous pretensions
Of those who are bent on upending everything
Till their egomanic vanity finally gleams
On the pinnacle
Of the abyss-turned-mountainpeak,

Beware, behind its radiant-beaming mask,
Beware above all in life
The envy
Of the envious who are angels.

XXXVII

When poor love cannot speak to tell its grief
Because the world, unpitying, hovers near
Mouthing banalities it loathes to hear
Through tedious aeons, granting no relief,

When, like a frail shell dashed upon a reef,
Its helpless gloom must strike the look severe
Of the fair idol who is doomed to sear,
With puzzled anger, wounds beyond belief,

Then suffering so madly multiplies,
With guessed misjudgement of its soundless cries
As sickness or perverse ungrateful spleen,
That it makes trivial even Calvary:

O my betrothed, what treasures might be seen
Could you but reach this heart's forbidden key.

XXXVIII

When I thee fail in love, it springs from this:
The world has interposed its killing triteness;
When I would pour my soul into a kiss,
Has pent me, ages-long, in cold politeness.

The world, in all its shallowness and shame,
Its insolence and falsity benighted,
Has murderously doused my lyric flame
And left my passion dumb and unrequited.

I need thee so much more than any other,
My child, my sister, bride and friend and mother,
That, when the arm that seeks thee must hang lonely

Or posture aimless for some stranger's pleasure
Through seeming lifetimes, be they minutes only,
It dies of grief, then cannot reach my treasure.

XXXIX

There is a place these eyes can hardly see,
Like a walled garden brimmed with blooms and sun
Where warm bees drone in gorged oblivion
While scent and colour surge abundantly;

Glimpsed through the lattice-gate it beckons me
To its effulgent heart, and there I run,
But envious weeds prevent our union
Barring me thence with every perfidy.

I almost reach it, then perforce retire
From stings and thorns that martyr my desire,
Flaunting their coarse and rancid mockery,
And thus they drain my tears and waste my powers;

Yet I, undaunted, scorn their enmity
For in my heart a kindred garden flowers.

XL

In this loud world where worthless words abound —
Words turned to flatter, or beslime, or maim,
Words that advance the sterile ego's claim,
And scourge those lives that gentle love has crowned —

Cannot we find some region without sound
Where bliss thrives needless of one uttered name,
Where we may tend our worship's precious flame
Like a shared altar set on hallowed ground?

Far from the trickle of corroding lies,
Far from the envies of less wholesome hearts,
Far from keen saboteurs and peering spies,
Far from contrivance and the serpent's arts,

Let us converse with balmful hands and eyes
And breasts and loins, and Cupid's noiseless darts.

XLI

When between you and one your soul adores
Each word that passes, although nobly meant,
Is thought to bear some sinister intent
Which your fair idol wincingly abhors;

When, maddened by this life's insistent sores,
Your dear love starts at every sentence spent
And you must tremble, waiting to dissent
From the disastrous inference she draws;

There is no course, except to wait and pray
That before long may dawn some calmer day
When the heart's message can attain its mark;

When she you worship, spared the din of pain
And terror's tumult, may unhindered hark
To changeless truth and draw you close again.

XLII

When in black spleen the soul, dejected, ploughs
And words cannot be kept upon their course
Though true love, weeping, heaves their truant prows,
How bitter, and how helpless, the remorse.

How dire the need for looks compassionate
And not some stern, unpitying reprimand;
I know I wounded, in my wounded state,
But grant my butchered heart your salving hand.

If tears can wash away the taint of gall
Then tide enough has flowed since my offence,
And I have grief enough for bathing all
I ever harmed, in briny recompense.

I pray then, mercy flow from you no less
And soothe the sombre depths of my distress.

XLIII

Lovers are heroes whom both Gods and men,
Angels and minions, envy and oppose;
With every joy a venomed anger grows
As Eden pours its wriggling denizen.

With arts beyond his dreaming victims' ken,
The snake whom hatred twists in hideous throes
Plots a new Hell where spotless ardour glows,
Hatching up discord in his devious den.

He whispers first to her and then to him
Deft-tinted half-truths well designed to dim
The radiant vision each in each beholds,
And spits his blackest gall before their eyes.

But when trust's mantle blends them in its folds
Lovers can crush all foes, and pierce all lies.

XLIV

Let us hold firm, though dire in its resolve
The world beleaguers beauty, love and bliss,
Aching to breach the fortress of our kiss
And in loud strife our harmonies dissolve;

Though writhing foes on every hand revolve
Their venomed plans, though hatreds round us hiss
Their faceless threat of hideous nemesis,
And intrigues taunt us that no wit may solve,

Let us hold firm, and if the very mind
Succumbing in our siege, can neither hear
Nor formulate that message calm and kind
Wherewith in health we one another cheer,

Let us hold firm, and with one girdle bind
Our sacred troth, of all in life most dear.

XLV

In the first days of heaven-granted grace
I waved my noble banner over love
Determined to defend its Eden grove
From the foul earthling and his grimy trace.

But, once bliss blooms, a million envies race
To the presumptuous spot and strive to prove
Both idols false that could such worship move
And daub their shrine with grossness commonplace.

Professing motives radiant as the skies
The wreckers sow distrust with choicest lies
And watch clear features clouding at their words.

Poor victims who found solace each in each,
How soon were we destroyed by sullying speech,
And joined the snakes, though we were soaring birds.

XLVI

O worst of hells, to fail one's most beloved
Through dire exhaustion with a train of deeds
That strove and strove again to tend her needs,
Then end one's days rejected and reproved.

To serve, with bursting heart, her cause alone
With rarest vigour lashed by rarer will
Like a fine steed its rider's spurs can kill,
And then to fall from glorious motion prone.

To find in her one's purpose and one's pride,
To gain in stature with the strenuous hours,
To prove one's troth with superhuman powers
Then feel the poor mind stagger in its stride.

To reel in feeble folly at the last
And blunder, while her pain blots out the past.

Godboot

After the hour when happiness is radiant
And for some favoured one or two at least
Humanity sheds its taint and undertow
And becomes as if divine,
At peace with self and setting,
Poised on a mountaintop of attainment,
Gliding for a blissful space in harmony
Through noiseless ethers of pure altitude
After the toil and torment of ascent,
Stealing only one moment,
One goblet of crystal ecstasy,
One rush of a waterfall over a lofty brink,
One kiss of crest and fleecy passing vapour,
One worshipful glance at human beauty alone
Which answers once with angelic radiance,

Always, after the briefest interval,
That acres-broad, tons-heavy hobnailed boot
Of the self-laudatory jealous Jewish God,
Hater of beauty, lovers, and every smile,
Arch-enemy of the species he *claimed* to create,
Comes crashing down crushingly out of a cloudless sky;
And, like stamped-on worms,
The happy shrink, recoil
Making no sound at that sudden explosion of pain,
Rebuking with muteness that insensitive giant
Whose vindictive egotism cannot hear.
Then, as the numbness induced by the battering fades,
Curling up slowly in our agony,
We discover the power of movement once again
    And try, try to ascend.

XLVII

Believing most in you, and least in me:
My heart in spate with words that will not flow,
My understanding ill-designed to know
The message of your heart's abundancy;

Doomed to lie quaking in the dismal cell
Of my own fears and fate's anathemas,
To see your beauty as through prison-bars,
To dote on heaven and yet rot in hell,

This is how I, who hurt you, suffer hurt
In those dread moments when the hero halts
On life's arena, shattered by the chase;

When trailing garlands still, of just desert,
I ponder helpless on my mound of faults
And watch while scorn invades your grieving face.

XLVIII

O ache of knowing that I cause you pain,
O pain you bring me though you mean it not,
O hell of learning that a heaven can rot
In the tart acid of a world's disdain.

There came a goddess once like gentle rain
And gentler mercy; my most blessed lot
Her stintless worship while the heart forgot
Quotidian nausea and quotidian stain.

But mean fate waited with its fund of time
And baseless pit of plots to bring us down
For daring thus to limn a golden clime
That set the very hosts of bliss a-frown.

Our spotless flame was dimmed by slander's slime
Though tears were kindled fit to jewel a crown.

IL

There was a world of gentleness and calm
And radiance and warmth and harmony,
Of blending hands, and eyes whose brilliancy
Held firmaments of bliss beyond all harm.

There was a place where confidence and trust
Reposed and were in solemn gift exchanged,
And life's grotesque distortions rearranged
Or banished from its haven in disgust.

There was such beauty that the envious herd
Choked on its implications of disdain,
Hating this challenge to their modish reign
Which issued without gesture, without word.

There was a glory where now dwells but pain
Of two glad gods that mortals made insane.

L

There is a shrine wherein a figure kneels
Who has not stirred from kneeling during years:
It is your image that he so reveres;
Only for you, with all that's his, he feels.

Across his anguished back run scarlet weals
Where impious fate has laid a lash that sears,
And through his long delirium's hell he hears
The rain of lies that slanderous envy deals.

From the fair idol pulsing crimson flows
While the nave trembles to her pain-mad cries,
And with each pang her cutting hatred grows
For the bowed figure who with tears replies.

Another scream: blood-bright your eikon glows;
Another rending thong: blood scalds my eyes.

LI

O clash of arms where would be clasp of hands,
O glare of fury where sweet fire still burns,
O gash of cruel words where kindness yearns,
O aching void where neither understands.

O hell of distance when the heart still cleaves,
O rain of tears that quenches peerless sun,
O tragic close of that in bliss begun,
O travesty when reverence raves and leaves.

These have we known in days our darkest yet
When all the arsenals of fate were trained
Upon the envied scene of earthly heaven.

These have o'ercast our skies with drapes of jet,
These have our mountains' pristine waters stained,
These may we fight with love's untiring leaven.

LII

Drawn tense to breaking on the rack of fate,
Scanning the empty heavens for a friend,
Watching the clouds converge to spend their spate
On the trussed human form no shreds defend;

With gutted pupils raised in helpless hate
At lightning thongs that ruthlessly descend,
With heart all tremblous that unknowing must wait
In its dark cage for vicious pangs to rend;

Robbed of all power to fight the cosmic foe
Whom nothing will placate and nothing move,
My worst of anguish being that I know

You near me suffer and I cannot prove
My timeless care except by tears' mute flow,
Through howling hell I plead my voiceless love.

LIII

Nothing will change, although the world has schemed
To taint and to diminish what we knew,
This heart is more than ever laved in you
And all we ever shared and ever dreamed.

Nothing will change, although the murderous crime
Of those who take, not paltry life, but love
Has by fate's means and minions seemed to prove
Its power to drown us in the tide of time.

Nothing will change, because the soul that speaks
These pounding words whose echoes will not die
Shall cling to them like a reverberant sigh
Renewing its passion as the brine that breaks.

Nothing will change, through all the stifling years,
This breast where wells not blood but blended tears.

LIV

I call to thee across an empty world
Where shades I scarcely see walk heedless by;
They do not hear my soul's unaltering cry
That is for thy true essence only hurled.

I call to thee across the wastes of hell
With all I ever strove to be and do;
Sad aspirant, whose passion rarely knew
The bliss of shielding her he worshipped well.

It was not want of valour nor of will
That brought us down: unyielding fate contrived
That love should fail, and puny foes connived.

We meet and touch no more, but still and still
In some dimension that I pray meets thine
I call to thee, a suppliant for a sign.

LV

The streets are filled with emptiness — your face
Flits constantly and always vanishes;
What my hope summons, then my dire disgrace
In having hurt you straightway banishes.

I see you everywhere, each time in vain,
For into alien features yours are changed;
Endless recurrence of my loss and pain,
As hearts I dream re-met are re-estranged.

I wronged you and I did not spare the wrong,
Yet what I did was as a helpless slave,
A suffering witness of the hateful throng
Of demons torturing that love I crave.

O grief-struck soul, to whom these tears I tell.
Return in truth and lead me from this Hell.

LVI

Reality's a slum: I shall not dwell
Between its stained and pestilential walls,
Where the obscene befouling insect crawls
And fairest love is doomed to fiercest hell;

No, I shall burst from that abysmal cell
Where hatred cankers and the rabble brawls,
And in the land of dream that gently calls
Will build my heart its golden citadel.

No carping envy shall approach me there,
No coarseness craze with curst proximity:
Serene and proud and stately I shall stare
Across my sumptuous realm's infinity;

And yet how void would be that shimmering air
Without your presence and your radiancy.

Day's End
(a Baudelairean linked pantun)

The sun sinks angry with a rage I share,
Empurpled mists withhold me from the hills
Where heaven throve awhile mid mortal ills,
And now a dark shroud seals up my despair.

Empurpled mists withhold me from the hills,
Heights where we fled the herd on wings of air,
And now a dark shroud seals up my despair
Though I fought nightfall with the king of wills.

Heights where we fled the herd on wings of air
Now languish neath a stifling veil that chills,
Though I fought nightfall with the king of wills
I scarce can breathe to whisper that I care.

Now languish neath a stifling veil that chills
The pulses of the heart you heard me bare,
I scarce can breathe to whisper that I care
Though all the crimsoned sky with anguish fills.

LVII

How can I say, when such a harm is done,
I meant you only tenderness and joy,
A respite from life's ills together won,
An Eden whose delights would never cloy?

How can I say, when such a wound is given,
I wanted but to cradle and to praise
A heart that here on earth brought very heaven
And green abundance to my desert ways?

Tears drench these orbs as I behold the page
And palsied is my pen with trembling nerves,
At fate and pain and lunacy I rage
And the bleak sureness that no plea now serves.

Grotesque and hopeless, but till death still true,
Within this jagged wreck I worship you.

LVIII

Schism of psyche, curse of western man
Since he forswore his Grecian harmony,
Gulf between heart and soul, so hard to span,
Could even our rich-hued love not vanquish thee?

If fate had been our friend, if others' eyes
Had not been mean and hateful of our bliss,
Should we have turned insane with fouling lies
And veered and wounded though we craved to kiss?

Would our fond need, without this blast of ice,
This draught of envious death that spurred our fire,
Have cast so recklessly its dangerous dice
Until love's spirit censured love's desire?

We should have drawn together with one shawl
Two doting creatures and each other's all.

LIX

Well, Fate, thou blind and blundering wrecker, hast
Thou done thy worst and trod our glory down?
Where there was wonder must we cringe aghast?
Where there was worship must we curse and frown?

Where there was shelter from the scourging blast
Must a grim, fissured ruin moan and drown?
Must lover from beloved be torn at last
And each glad god be made thy weeping clown?

There is one sanctum thou canst not defile,
There is one casket thou shalt never breach
Which holds each poignant sigh, each crystal smile
And every soft enlacement's tremorous speech —

All the heart's will, unstained by worldly guile,
Locked, while men breathe and read, beyond thy reach!

LX

We are frail polyps, and our pearly reef
The art that builds as each brave life is spent,
Proof that we wrought well though our flower was brief
And in us bore some undissolved intent.

The radiant hour may die, love writhe in grief,
And earthly joys bring wrathful chastisement,
Yet the heart's hope, heart's worship, heart's belief
Scorn to be altered by what fate has sent.

In strife that some fine essence shall endure
Beyond all vengeance by an envious doom,
Some flawless remnant at our sculpted core,
We fashion, when we can, a surer bloom;

And your rare beauty in my song's proud score
Branches and gleams despite the battering spume.

LXI

Through all that comes, remember one sweet night
When with our sonnets and our true love's power
We gleaned from time our every tenderest hour
And grew still tenderer as we held them tight.

I heard your frail and tremblous tones recite
Each line your beauty nurtured into flower,
And all the blossoms of our Eden's bower
Triumphed anew in sullen Fate's despite.

Rare wonder, that two mortals should enshrine
This universe of harmony and bliss
Which all the ills of Man cannot confine.

Shall other souls, like ours, more bravely shine
From the clear jewels enkindled when we kiss?
And does all heaven rejoice in yours and mine?

LXII

Though Beatrice by marriage-vows was barred
From fragile hope, and Death — more final still —
Made her his bride and bowed her to his will,
Dante wrote on, still eloquent if scarred.

And Petrarch, though his plight was no less hard
In harbouring love he never could fulfil,
Penned Laura sonnets of unfading skill
When plague had reft him of his fair De Sade.

So too may I, though fate and foe have stained
The purest dream that this stale earth retained,
Fight mid the trash and tinsel of our age
To voice your beauty and my undimmed flame,

To curse our saboteurs with quenchless rage
And steep their baseness in a slough of shame.

LXIII

If on some distant shore these frail words spill
Like droplets from the ocean of my grief,
And find some breed that knows at last relief
From the crass herd now fostering art so ill;

If, by some feat of fortune and of will,
These offspring of an ardour fair as brief
Reach a proud age that kindles new belief
In noble hearts adorned with courtly skill;

Then may they speak to ears that comprehend
Of you and me, and all that we endured
From the gross barbs of devious enmity
Which wounded love until it could not mend;

May they give voice till stately spheres applaud
My faithful plume, your unbowed majesty.

LXIV

A supple swallow who was wont to flute
The spacious air in his mercurial flight
And well could give and well evade pursuit
Was found one day aground in desperate plight.

Too ill to stir, he lay distraught and mute
While over his poor plumage, once so bright,
Spread, like a slander he could not refute,
The dark hordes of some insect-parasite.

So was it when, in love's sweet sickness, we
Permitted all who sought our warmth to throng
And nestle in our magnanimity.

Too late, we found their envy wrought our wrong,
Marauded, loaded, used us ruthlessly,
And paralysed our flight, and stilled our song.

LXV

Heroic rose, thus long have you prevailed
Against the withering rime that grips the ground,
Like a pale blight on curls by age assailed,
To warn that we're for lethal winter bound.

Brave rose, still radiant in this fading scene,
Emblem of hope to my imperilled heart,
You blazon all the glories that have been
Upon the dearth if she and I should part.

Speak to her, rose, as you have done to me,
Speak to her through these lines I send her now:
Tell with what dread I wrought each injury,
Tell her what worship gleams yet on my brow,

Plead that she pardon him whom anguish sears,
Who staggers with her wounds, who sobs her tears.

LXVI

You shed your petals, rose, while I shed tears:
Your message to her heart has brought no thaw;
Winter is conquering, you can thrive no more,
And fate now mocks my love with impious jeers.

Far is that warm spring when I blossomed first
And tore the sheathing membrane from my breast,
That as her need desired her brow might rest
In tenderness though hazard did its worst.

Bare to the blast, I tremble like a flower
That cannot cheer her mid the wastes of pain;
She hates that sweet place where her dreams have lain
That seem so false now through time's altering power;

And though they blush their worship for her still
My palsied remnants slowly wilt and spill.

LXVII

Street of the Stairs, thou ancient cobbled rise,
Too many moons ago I brought to thee,
One azure night of star-bejewelled skies,
My heart's sweet choice for all eternity.

As to some honoured ancestor she came,
With eager diffidence and tremblous pride,
So often had she heard me speak thy name;
And when her beauty witnessed thine, she cried.

Hushed was thy valley, silvered every form,
With pools of shadow where I held her near;
The shielding church and cresting school were warm
With benedictions, staunching every fear.

O life, O fate, would time had never moved
From that blest moment when we stood and loved.

LXVIII

Some blissful day, when glory gilds the air
And love thrives in our glance and tryst of hands,
When the heart's mercy soothes and understands,
And fate relents, and saboteurs despair,

Shall we return to seek that cloister's shade,
Those tranquil walks through groves of branching stone
Past glazen saints where, to the silvery tone
Of evensong, our pristine vows were made?

Shall we draw close once more in dusk's soft shawl
And share sweet grace and silent thankfulness
And, blest of heaven, in each other bless
The soul divine, beneath that holy pall;

Shall each confess that in the other's heart
Is the best haven — God's alone apart?

LXIX

The storm had wakened me to solitude
In the bleak desert of a cheerless night
Through whose cold plains a peevish wind pursued
With vicious lash some foe in hectic flight.

My house clung trembling to its grassy bed
As though the whim of some delirious horde
With bloodlust roused and every scruple shed
Might seize and raze it to the shivering sward.

And in that solitude with all plucked bare
About me — combed, uprooted, fallen, crushed —
A single truth held firm, a single care
Which still calls clearly now the storm has hushed:

Your warmth, your mercy, and my heart's wild need
To bide in yours — its haven and its creed.

LXX

After long banishment of heart from heart
By the importunate weak that plague our age
Who force us to maintain an alien part
Like captive gods that pace a noisome cage;

After each gently-fostered protégé —
Responding not with gratitude but hate —
Has chosen, like leering Judas, to betray
A loftier species to a crippling fate;

After the blank-eyed tyrant of routine
Has numbed our being with his foot-worn mill
Until we scarce recall what we have been
And scale, it seems, a never-ending hill;

After this exile, some refulgent day
Let me come home to you. Tell me I may.

LXXI

I am a dreamer — yes, you have it right —
Of dreams that distant ancestry has spawned,
Grandiose distinctions by the masses scorned
And vanished now in dense plebeian night.

I am a dreamer, yet my dearest prayer
Was ever to have earned some present praise,
To deck my temples with unfaded bays
And homeward bear my prize, and find you there.

I am a dreamer, yet with all my will
I strove to steer the reckless barque of fate
Towards the haven of a happier state
When we were safe from all that wrought us ill.

I am a dreamer, but my dreams met you,
And loved in truth, and battled to come true.

LXXII

I strode the lane where we had walked before
When Nature teemed and ardour thrilled the air.
The farm lay wintering: its fields were bare
Of crops and herds; its eaves no longer bore

Those milky doves that made the heart so sure
Of shared felicity and steadfast care.
Again, again I went, in gnawing despair
To find no life about the cote's trim door.

Then, like a Christmas gift from coming Spring,
A cloudless day unfurled its azured wing,
And drew me once more to that treasured place.

While still far off I glimpsed the pearly flame
That grew to one bright couple, merged in grace;
And all the heavens kindled to your name.

LXXIII

This misted landscape with envaulting trees
That in their veiled gradations subtly fade
Towards some distant and elusive glade
Whose screen is bright with mystic lucencies

Enthrals my gaze, recalls lost ecstasies
When I have stood entranced as Nature laid
Her cloudy mantle round me and dismayed
My spirit with her minster's pieties:

All the small rites in broader day unknown —
Tremor of stalk or leaf, or crystal bead,
Or jewelled gossamer — for me alone
Were wrought by unseen hands that knew my need;

But now my rapt heart sings in richer tone
And prays a human altar pays it heed.

LXXIV

Around the unturned corner of our fate
Is there some house that waits, deserted, gaunt,
Which only shadows of the future haunt
Beyond the blank panes of its lifeless state?

Is there some garden, spurned and desolate,
With neither fruit nor flower left to flaunt,
A riot of defiant weeds that daunt
Beyond the stiff hinge of its rotting gate?

And shall we turn that corner of our way,
Despite all pains and hardships, hand-in-hand,
And see that lonely ruin turn straightway
To pearl and crystal, by your magic scanned?

And shall we enter, laugh and weep and pray
On the light threshold of our promised land?

LXXV

Not too many eternities away,
When fate has wearied of its urge to maim
And love revives its anguish-riven flame,
Come to my heart, come to my heart and stay.

All that is in this breast on that sweet day
Your all, if it so honour me, shall claim
And I shall worship, weeping without shame,
And I shall riot, reckless in our play.

All the world's chill and distance then shall die,
All the world's tedium, falsity and strain,
When we are smile to smile and eye to eye
And soft lips touch and soft limbs twine again,

When we are gods once more and own the sky
And in each other's bounteous Eden reign.

LXXVI

If, in the cycles of slow time, should rise
Renaissance of our love, despite grave harm;
If we can draw together, balm to balm,
And the heart grant and find its peerless prize.

If, at the deep oases of your eyes,
My own may drink that yearning shall grow calm;
If I may take your hand, and palm to palm
Speak soft assurance of enduring ties.

If we may share the velvet nave of night
And in luxurious vastness voice our care
With eloquence of touch that rains delight,
With kiss and tear that lay devotion bare;

If I may clasp you far from harsh affright
And blend one ballet in the angeled air!

LXXVII

Fate had bereft me of what most I craved,
What most I strove for and what most revered;
Of all the reckless wonders that endeared
It seemed, by then, that nothing could be saved.

Like one from whom life ebbed, I saw again
Each scene that in our springtide we had shared;
All the bright strokes that mid grey life we dared
Shone now like braziers kindled for my pain.

Half-crazed, I spoke your name through dismal days
A thousand times, embroidering their void
While strangers started, puzzled and annoyed
By this fierce ripple in their level ways;

Until I heard your voice's gracious leaven
That is for me the very heart of heaven.

LXXVIII

Skies had been barred from me by riftless cloud
Of ritual whence the life and joy had fled;
My days crept onward with unvarying tread,
My eyes stared empty at their clinging shroud.

My vault was locked, its precious golden key
Withdrawn and all that lustre plucked away;
My dusty tongue lay still and could not pray,
My pained heart's pulse had paused dejectedly.

Then, unannounced as sunshine, you arrived
And summoned me with light so that I rose
And soared with you in ways your magic chose
And watched and wondered as lost glories thrived.

Your blessing bathed me, and my dazzled gaze
Travelled your bounteous face in pride and praise.

LXXIX

One word across the voids of space and time,
If sprung from you, transmutes my dross to gold;
One word, sweet riches for my heart to hold,
And out of depths that had no end I climb.

I need not hear your voice nor see your pen,
Provided that the source as yours I know
Which feeds my sullen ocean with its flow,
To cheer my brine with pristine drops again.

The weariness of dull quotidian things
Falls from me then, the petty loses all
Its power to stun me and to stay my wings;

I shed the cage where lackeys leer and crawl
And, pride restored, my spirit soars and sings,
Scaling the heavens, calling with your call.

LXXX

I meet you, loved one, though the world unkind
Has taught a harshness to our grieving ways,
Has told us silken threads are thongs that bind
Or the heart's tender need a beast that preys.

I meet you, loved one, though an envious sky
Has watched our Eden, wishing we were foes,
Planting the snake to twist our trust awry
Till the bared breast was weak with wounding blows.

I meet you, loved one, though the pulse grown frail
Set hands all tremblous on the cooling wrist,
Till silence teemed with fears that we should fail
And only kindred terrors touched and kissed.

I meet you, loved one, as the summer dies
And find the spring, resurgent in your eyes.

LXXXI

Yes, there is still a heaven: in your eyes,
Your smile, your touch, your banter, and your love;
A heaven still, and jealous distance lies
In telling of a dearth your looks disprove.

When we are exiled from each other's sight,
Long parted by the tasks that nail us down,
Despair's dense clouds too easily alight
About the brow, and veil it in a frown.

My fears are bottomless when, far from you
I brood upon my goals, and though I hear
The loveliest voice on earth, the fondest too,
Your being slowly fades, till you are near.

But then, what riches! From my cell forlorn
I burst and worship, vibrant and reborn.

LXXXII

To look into your eyes and know of love;
That though our very species be absurd
Our ardour's gift is not, that but one word
Between us shared can chime the spheres above.

To know that we are home, whatever trek
Between our first and final pulse is planned;
That heaven is the shrine wherein we stand
And give our hearts in worship none can check.

We have arrived, we have come through the test
By fate and foe and Providence assigned;
What strove to rend apart has served to bind,
And garland you Earth's loveliest and best.

And eyes and hands and lips now softly meet
And in eternal time two breasts now beat.

LXXXIII

It is astounding: time had ticked us on
So deftly, as it ticks the year from spring,
The fabled flower from birth to withering
And the proud hour of being to oblivion.

We spoke in prose now, love's wild trance had gone
And words had caught a sane and sober ring;
Our ritual-ridden race had schemed to bring
Us, chained, to its grey self, and it had won.

Dictating to our days, and wresting smiles
To order in the brothel of blank toil,
It had left little of ourselves to plight
Where we would plight it, fond and free of wiles.

Then from your plain thoughts, planted in my soil,
All your heart's beauty surged and throbbed with light.

LXXXIV

When I scan lucent skies or vibrant stars,
When kindness melts the glacier of my day,
When through this race of pallid nenuphars
There ripples fleetingly some golden ray;

When I find ease after abrasive toil,
When I glimpse beauty through the gargoyle herd,
When I taste grandeur that no churl can spoil
I utter then a single thankful word.

For over the engulfing slough that clings,
The acid-bite of malice, barb of hate,
One fine ethereal presence round me wings
Rekindling will and visions that elate,

One face, one heart, both lovely, to whose fame
These lines are plighted; and they bear your name.

LXXXV

There is a sanctuary in this fraught world,
By our crazed fallen race made desolate,
Whereinto you and I, by some blind fate,
With scant attention to our will, were hurled.

Through the grim trampling millions, knaved and churled,
Bristling with envy, avarice, and hate,
I always glimpse that tranquil shrine await
And feel a cloak of refuge being unfurled.

Blest without stint, thus stintless I revere
An altar which at every call will hear;
Its beauties dazzle my poor human eye
Stricken with guilt at tending it so ill.

How wondrous is your heart. O would that I
With kindred solace might its chancel fill.

LXXXVI

Are all the travels of Odysseus done?
After the storms and perils near and far
And snaring webs by fiendish intrigue spun
Am I come home at last to Ithaca?

There is no warmth and constancy like yours
No mercy like that reigning in your breast,
And can I enter now with brine-bleached oars
Your waiting harbour at our love's behest?

I would that every day might end like this,
That from its tedious round I might retrieve
The timeless wonder of your smile and kiss;

That every night our limbs might interweave
A never-ending braided tapestry,
And I o'erride you like a silken sea.

LXXXVII

Be my heart's home, with every door flung wide,
Your arms and lips and loins my harbour sure;
At each day's end let me for solace draw
To your sweet port and from life's tumult hide.

I have an aching need which fretted pride
Can ill conceal and only you can cure;
Your soothing voice and tending hand restore
This weary vessel strained by wind and tide.

Within your haven dwells another world
Where all is peace, and tortured sails are furled,
And the racked hull rocks gently like a child;

And for your blessing as you bring me rest,
For sweet response to ministrations mild,
My breast's truth shall be spoken to your breast.

LXXXVIII

The tears come easier now, for truth's rare wound
Is opened, aching deep, and bleeding clean;
I am no more the waxen might-have-been
In the lost past and stifled self marooned.

A caring heart has sought me and attuned
My life to hers: the sightless soul has seen;
The locks are shattered of my dungeon-spleen
And in her rays' delirium I have swooned.

Our glances cross, and at that meeting-place
Such light abides as blinds the universe:
All tenderness, all honour, and all grace
Dwell shimmering there though Fates and Furies curse;

I pour my love towards that wondrous face
And, as I weep, God's salving streams immerse.

LXXXIX

There is a heroine I wreathe in praise
Who, though the envious stars have wrought her harm,
Cheers all about her with unfaltering charm
And with her warmth brings wonder to my days.

She leads my heart with hers in hallowed ways
Where memory's gentle fingers work their balm,
Where love, despite unfriendly fate, grows calm
And my devotion's lyre mellifluous plays.

And it is she, my Goddess and my Muse,
Whose image motions every breath I draw
And shines upon the night above my prayer.

Dear Heaven, for mercy's sake do not refuse
To that sweet breast whence tender bounties pour
Its long deferred release from cruel despair.

XC

To drink your every tear into my breast,
To kiss your every pore with burning lips,
To thrill each nerve with tremblous fingertips,
To soothe all pain of life and bring you rest;

To share mid silken sheets delirious zest
Of still more silken limbs, to fuse our hips
With throbbing life while truth's compulsion grips,
To be one heart, possessing and possessed:

Thus I portray that dream wherefore we grieve
Of the wild moment when all veils are shed
And what is dearest found and formed afresh;

When the mean world relents and grants us leave
To brim with reckless bliss our marriage bed
And utter all the love in heaven, made flesh!

XCI

Tell me, do you in torrid moments crave
To drain my worship through each thirsting pore,
Lie in the starfish pose my lips adore
And taste their pizzicati till you rave?

Do you sprawl prostrate like some vanquished slave
And dream you rule me with your lithe allure,
With shapely contours that have power to draw
Desire in chains, as moons will haul the wave?

I pray you do, for tremblous I confess
The madness of my need to touch your heart
By every course your tempting form provides,

To ring love's countless changes as I bless
Your wondrous all through every perfect part
With you, the best of goals, my best of guides.

XCII

Grant me my Darling with her curls drawn high
In Roman pride and frank audacity,
Her all for my delirious kiss made free
From slender wincing nape to sumptuous thigh.

Grant me her ear's frail shell where sounds the sigh
Of amorous oceans loitering wistfully;
Grant me her spine whose every tremblous key
Awaits arpeggios that will burst the sky.

Grant me her bareback and unreined desire
That coyly feigns indifference to my fire
And hugs the pillow to provoke me more!

Grant that beneath my craving she may craze
Then slowly from her proneness turn in awe
To meet my reverent eyes with hers ablaze!

XCIII

The mists of distance part and now your smile
Restores me and your warm gaze bathes my heart,
And I am yours without reserve or guile —
My love in your love framed as at the start.

I worship mid your mercy's radiance now
More humbly than first fervour could have dreamed,
Your stars with brighter rapture guide my prow,
More surely sail I home since storms have screamed.

In one bland harmony we blend and glide
And clasp and ease ourselves and clasp anew,
Sob in the throes of kisses long denied,
Whisper and laugh through tears that it is true —

We to whom hostile fortune proved a friend,
Testing our ardour till it could not end.

XCIV

I am an aesthete and a lover too,
And all the hosts of stern Malvolian gloom
That cast on taste and zest their blighting doom
Won't keep me now from beauty or from you.

Sometimes I veer as they would have me do
And leave my body like a vacant room,
Our lavish bed as cheerless as the tomb
Where your despair condemns me for untrue.

But faint not at their thin-toned clarion
That made of me our strange apostate foe;
Ancestral shades must pale where you have shone
And the chill clouds this dreadful challenge know:

That whomsoever Love has joined as one
Let no lone prophet part with envious blow.

XCV

Come to my racing heart, and let us rove
The tide of our tumultuous nights unknown,
Sharing a passion whence all veils are thrown
And in delirium perfect partners prove.

Let your bright orbs flash beckoningly above,
Your breast like buoyant brine sustain my own,
Your arms be shrouds that hold me trimly prone,
Your hips my helm that steers me into love.

There let me plunge and plunge my virile bows,
Your cries the liquid echo that I rouse
With every thrust through wave on flexing wave.

There let my madness in your own be drowned,
There let us kiss and weep and laugh and rave!
There let our all be lost, our all be found.

XCVI

Take me aboard those broad-beamed hips of yours
And let me row your regal barge in style,
At your fair pleasure plunging deep my oars
Or pausing as contentment glides awhile.

When you flex buoyant on a silken tide
Those rakish lines that rouse my gallantry,
Answer each manly thrust that drives with pride
Your snow-white prow of swanlike majesty.

May we for utmost harmony then aim
Where straining crew and stately vessel blend,
I in your beauty, you my fervour's flame,
As potent rhythm builds and strokes extend.

Till, when we triumph together in the race,
Our bold hearts fuse in an enspumed embrace!

XCVII

Triumph in life brings triumph to our love:
Our warm eyes meet and melt in amorous haze,
Proud ardour hastens to give thanks and praise,
And suave denuding hands like oceans move.

Your deft caresses gaily weave and rove,
Kindling my glory with their witching ways
Till, like a well-rigged galleon, I raise
Full crest of sail before I make your cove.

I glide to berth in smooth tranquillity,
Hailed by your anchoring kiss and tight embrace;
And when I seize you hard to ride and rive

Your fond loins cling in turn, containing me
With clasp of calves that cross and interlace —
And in that garland heroes' passions thrive!

XCVIII

Like a nude Goddess in some soaring dream
Of rapt baroque who scales a lofty dome
With buoyant ease and elegance supreme,
Seeming the very vaults of heaven to comb,

So you, my Love, who glide serenely bare
Through our Elysium's wispy draperies,
Swept by caresses smooth as fleeting air,
In your most pleasure most your servant please.

I'm like the very painter of your form,
Moulding its moods and postures while you fly
Through spacious shimmering calm or amorous storm,
With strange new vistas staggering the eye;

Drawn by your charm, fresh charms from you I draw
And, as my hand portrays, my lips adore.

IC

To thank you for your heart's abundancy
Let me some night lay bare your every pore
And without stint of rhetoric adore
Each pliant contour of your nudity.

Let me like some rude pantheist of old
Worship each peak, each hill, each knoll, each dell,
Each warm and sheltering vale, each sacred well,
Till to your all my message has been told.

Let me from nape to instep lead my train
Of pilgrim kisses by a host of ways
Twixt shrine and shrine where rapturous delays
Rouse answering tremors in your soft terrain.

And when you are replete and nothing lack
Be thankful in return, and kiss me back!

C

One bed that holds us in a swoon divine,
A single flesh, a single reverie,
A single rite that blends a trinity —
Our nudity, our kisses, and our wine.

One hand that ministers, while limbs entwine
And lock in love, one hand left nimbly free
To serve, as lips desire, now you, now me —
A single celebrant, a single shrine.

A single wrist that shares a single grace,
A single worship, of and in your face
That is sweet angel's and meek acolyte's.

A single heaven and a single soul,
A single heart-beat, echoed by the night's —
One joy, one measureless and boundless whole.

CI

Oh I have kissed the bronze coins at your breasts
And circled them with sleek seducing tongue
And gently sucked and gripped them till were sprung
In ripe response their firm erectile crests.

Oh I have kissed your feet like fragile birds
Trapped by my palms and in a swoon of fear,
Until they grew in trust and learnt how dear
Their tenderness from hymns that had no words.

Oh I have kissed your wincing nape and spine,
Soft inner thigh, neat navel, loins divine.
And revelled in the storm that thence would burst.

But I have kissed your lips a thousand ways,
With lightest love-touch or till lungs conversed,
And here I set my heart, and proudest praise.

CII

I love the little sounds you make in sleep
From that most private world I lie beside,
Holding your suave form close in tranquil pride
While your mind drifts in oceans dark and deep.

Within your velvet night I raptly steep
All consciousness and through your fathoms glide;
Grace interblends the contours of our tide
And whispers to this vigil that I keep.

But when you wash onto the shelving shore
Of gradual waking, and one amorous hip
Steals to its comrade as fond fingers draw

The blanket barrier from their fellowship,
What harmony and warmth are ours, what awe
As twin souls into one glad body slip.

CIII

Though the day's creaking mill may wear the mind
And grind our golden words to platitudes,
Crushing our grandeur till it bleeds and broods,
Let not your heart nor mine be made less kind.

Heard messengers may falter and may fail
To pass from breast to breast their burden fond,
But those unheard can voice a deeper bond,
More rich, more vibrant, on their soundless scale.

Their cunning has not fled, that subtler verve
Of fluttering eyelash or of printing lip,
Of whirlpool tongue or ferrying fingertip
That draws cool currents through your every nerve;

And down my spine still echoes the refrain
Of one mute might, renewing your timeless reign.

CIV

Now that our hearts in such rich hues combine
Like a full-spectrumed arc lit bright through rain,
With all once mine now yours, all yours now mine,
We can make love both sacred and profane.

That piety so tender and so grave
Whose kisses were like prayers or hymns of praise
Still shall we interchange as in a nave
Where twin forms worship and twin candles blaze.

But let there, too, be laughter, pagan mirth
Delirious with the vine, the bounteous earth;
And you, its fairest orchard, flaunting bare
Your body's wondrous fruits in clusters proud —

A new, more coaxing Eve, who need not spare
Desire with which such varied tinctures crowd.

Ballade of the Rainbow

The sun, the fen, the greenery that springs
Have finished sponging at the downpour's tears;
The insect shows anew, the bird now wings
Toward the dishevelled tree the zephyr cheers,
And the horizon's leaden visage clears.
Then, straddling all that hillside rusty browned,
Making dull pools, bored rocks, with glints abound,
And midst a curious chiaroscuro set,
The sodden heavens' great horeshoe burgeons round,
Red, orange, yellow, green, blue, violet.

The mushroom's cone its parasol outflings
Which seems to mourn the spate that disappears;
In G the frog, in C the cricket sings;
And, blending its mute wonder as it nears,
Night leaves the gladdened earth to dreamy spheres.
Then, through that arch which must its skies astound,
There fleets a flock of mists whom fears confound;
The tower recedes, with vaporous veils now wet,
And the defeated sun dies, slowly drowned,
Red, orange, yellow, green, blue, violet.

While in clear air, whose wine elation brings,
Climbs the keen freshness of the azured meres
And the unhaltered foal's shrill neigh outrings,
The last sob of absconded daylight sears
The farthest depths of cloud with radiant spears.
And o'er those streams that suppliant willows bound,
O'er ochrous poplar, cherry sanguine-crowned,
In mystic calm that knows no tumult's threat,
Is seen to fade that flexless bow renowned,
Red, orange, yellow, green, blue, violet.

ENVOI

O thou, the heart where mine has succour found
Against the storm of fate that fearsome frowned,
When, angel that in dream appeared, we met
My wan gaze was in rainbow brilliance gowned,
Red, orange, yellow, green, blue, violet.

(From the French of Maurice Rollinat)

CV

Moderns will mock these lines I turn for you
But in advance I answer them with this:
They have not loved your beauties as I do,
They have not kindled at your peerless kiss;

They lack a model worth the praise of art,
They lack the bard's apprenticeship and skill,
And, more than this, they lack the constant heart
That holds to its beloved through good and ill.

They most of all, in this aberrant age,
Lack knowledge of the best that went before;
Their egoes froth in unperceptive rage
While the gold bâton tended . . . they ignore.

Such wealth that was, and is in what we share,
They slight with sneers that speak their own despair.

CVI

We toast 'the century', and those who hear
Imagine maybe that we toast their age,
Exulting to be set on such a stage
And with such actors and spectators near.

I hate to disabuse them, but our cheer
Derives from no such dubious privilege,
For we have fitter repertoires to pledge
Than in plebian circuses appear!

Our 'century' is one of subtlest song
Wrought by our plighted hearts through taxing years
Despite, and not because of, such as these;

An hundred sonnets now to you belong
Filled with our Eden frontiered with tears
And echoing to statelier centuries!

NOTES TO THE SONNETS

The 'Architecture' of the Sequence

The movement of the sequence is as follows. First is portrayed the meeting with the beloved, the rapture of first love and the deepening knowledge of each other, together with the vow to worship and serve (III), the formal proposal (X), the determination to protect love and the Beloved despite the vicissitudes of life. Then appear the challenges to love's happiness, at first nothing more serious than separation (XX-XXIII), which is followed by a rapturous celebration of shared tenderness when the lovers are able to meet (XXIV-XXXVI). But presently comes that more sinister and destructive menace which those who are divinely happy all too often have occasion to fear, namely the malevolent and dogged envy of other human beings and (it almost feels) of the very cosmos itself. Although the lovers at first express their resolve to resist this more serious challenge (XXXIX-XLIV), it presently brings about a crisis in which both the lovers suffer (and are even made to inflict) untold agonies and are brought to the point of despair and rupture. The poet resorts to art to eternize some of the more ecstatic moments of what he believes to be irretrievably lost (LIX-LXII), but concludes by rejecting these hollow reveries in favour of the earnest desire to win back his Beloved (LXV-LXX). This yearning refuses to die, grows stronger, and is finally crowned with triumph (LXXVII-LXXXIX), after which love and love-making are celebrated as never before (XC-CII).

Individual Sonnets, etc.

I: This first sonnet describes the moment when the author received a revelation of the extraordinary beauty and exceptional quality of his future Muse. Appropriately enough, this occurred when both had been listening to an illustrated lecture on Renaissance art.

II: There is a deliberate echo in this sonnet from Donne's poem, 'The Good Morrow', lines 6-7.

III: This sonnet owes much to the beautiful words of the traditional Anglican marriage service. Revealingly, this poem is chronologically the very first of the sequence. Its successor in the sequence, full of gratitude and reverence for the divine, and generous goodwill towards men, followed soon afterwards.

V: This sonnet was composed in answer to my Beloved's concern in case I was attracted by no more than her external beauty.

VII & VIII: Both these sonnets voice my determination to defend the precious gift of love in everyday life.

IX: Something of the same determination is expressed in this sonnet, which however records also details of a happy day when I rowed my Beloved on the Dee above Chester.

X: The final couplet of this sonnet reverts to the same theme of perseverance. It belongs here in the sequence, though written long after my formal proposal to my Beloved, made in the beautifully restored cloisters of St. Werburgh's Abbey, adjoining Chester Cathedral (see LXVIII, below).

XI & XII: These both express intense concern to safeguard love and to offer tender reassurance to the Beloved.

XIII & XIV: Here, although striking a pagan stance at the time of writing, I open my heart to the Christian God of my Beloved.

XVI: The reference in the last line is of course to Sidney's sequence to Lady Rich, 'Astrophel (or more properly Astrophil) and Stella'.

XXI: The 'dear-held day', still dear and honoured regularly at the time of editing these sonnets, was that date in the month when I proposed to, and was accepted by, my Beloved.

XXIX: Written after reading some of Sidney's sonnets, although the last line echoes that of a double sonnet by D'Annunzio which I translated some years ago.

XXX: My family, like my country, entered the twentieth century full of hope, with my grandfather Cllr. James Higson of Friarswood House (sometime of Chester, see note to LXVII) established as one of the leading citizens of Newcastle-under-Lyme. But in the minority that followed his death we were deprived by a grasping step-parent of our paternal inheritance, while the maternal inheritance from his father-in-law (invested by his eldest son and heir, my Uncle Willoughby, in an estate at Molo, Kenya) was lost when Willoughby died there prematurely in 1918 while my father (his brother Roland, who had intended to join him at Molo) was serving in France in the First World War. Thus we Higsons, so recently engaged in consolidating our position among the gentry, and boasting a link with the ancient and honourable house of the Barons Willoughby of Parham, were plunged instead into straitened and chastened circumstances like angels dashed from paradise.

XXXII, ln.2: The parallel between foliage and hair is also D'Annunzian. The image of white doves was probably suggested by those at Town Farm, Norley (see LXXII, below), rather than by other poets.

XXXIII-V: These sonnets relate to a certain unforgettable occasion, on which my Beloved showed the tenderest and deepest compassion imaginable.

The Envious Angels: The 'you' in this poem is of course not my Beloved, so often addressed in the sonnet sequence itself, but the reader who is personally warned of an all-too-prevalent phenomenon at this stage so that the appearance of sanctimonious envy in the narrative shall be the more dramatic.

XXXVIII: Feminine rhymes are generally thought of as producing a humorous effect, but here they are used to sound a note of defeat and anguish by breaking into the regular rhythm of the poem.

XLIII: The image of the snake in Eden is used here to portray not the Fiend, tempting lovers with forbidden fruit and knowledge, but an envious human being plausibly distorting truth and tainting beauty so as to destroy the harmony and radiance in which the lovers dwell. The image lingers in the two subsequent sonnets.

IL, ln.9: In a degenerate society envy grows increasingly prevalent, even that basest kind which resents and discourages intrinsically desirable characteristics like talent or industry. At such times, let those who possess the divine gift of honourable, constant, discriminating love be doubly on their guard!

LV, ln.1: The streets here referred to were those of Chester, teeming with human faces at the height of summer, but empty of the one I dearly wished to see.

LVI: Here I blatantly proclaim my intention to withdraw from detestable, vulgar, envy-ridden reality into my own private dream-world, but in the last two lines recall my poignant personal need for my Beloved. This conclusion was undoubtedly suggested by that of Lentini's best-known sonnet: *'Io m'agio posto in core a Dio servire . . .'*. The subsequent sonnets express insistent hope that the relationship can be repaired.

Day's End: This Baudelairean pantun virtually wrote itself after I had observed an angry sunset while walking on Chester city walls. It is clearly related to Baudelaire's beautiful poem, *'Harmonie du Soir'*, also motivated by a feeling of nostalgia for lost love.

LIX: In this bitter riposte against fate, which I believed at this stage to have destroyed my most cherished relationship, I contemptuously assert in the Renaissance manner that this wrecker will at least be unable to prevent the preservation of its memory through art.

LX: This sonnet, when published separately from the sequence, was entitled 'Coral', and the coral reef is here used as an image for defiantly eternizing art.

LXI: Here an occasion is recalled when, in a mood of great tenderness and harmony, we read to each other many of the sonnets which our love had produced.

LXII: Still on the theme of love's perpetuation by art, I affirm here that (in the manner of Renaissance sonneteers) I shall continue to praise the beauty of my Beloved even after I have lost her, and that I shall immortalize too the crimes of those who sought to undermine our happiness.

LXV: The late rose which was the starting-point of this sonnet was blooming in my own garden in late November. The final couplet is derived from that of No.XCIII in Sidney's sequence, 'Astrophel and Stella'. The Sonnet also obviously echoes Waller's 'Goe lovely Rose . . .', without presuming to vie with it.

LXVI: Inspired by the same rose as the preceding poem, when it began to shed in mid-December.

LXVII: The first of two more poems of nostalgia, this time associated with parts of Chester. The 'Street of the Stairs', as my Beloved and I have always called it after one in an adventure story which was a favourite of my youth (Adml. E.R.G.R. Evans & Draycott M. Dell, *The Treasure Trail*), is in fact St. Mary's Hill, one of the most unspoilt and picturesque corners of the City. Its 'cobbled rise' is flanked by St. Mary's-on-the-Hill Parish Church and is topped by the old St. Mary's School built in the 1840s. The place does indeed have ancestral associations as implied in the sonnet, for my grandfather James Higson (1839-1901), later Mayor of Newcastle-under-Lyme, attended the school c.1850 and must have toiled up the hill many times from the family home in Duke Street. My Beloved knew all about this, and about my very high regard for my grandfather, when I took her to this beautiful spot, which she had not visited before.

LXVIII: This sonnet, more hopeful of love's revival than its predecessor, recalls the time when I had proposed to my Beloved in the cloisters of the old abbey at Chester. The stained glass windows there depict for the most part famous saints, together with a few prominent leaders of the Anglican Church.

LXIX: The vicious storm which was the occasion for this poem swept my house in Newcastle-under-Lyme late one December.

LXX: While deploring the damage caused to our relationship by importunate dependants and exhausting routines, the poem prays for a renewal of harmony and this strengthening hope fills the sonnets that follow.

LXXII: This poem refers to a heartening experience I had when walking in the Cheshire countryside near Delamere Forest. The white doves were (and probably still are) kept at Town Farm, near Norley Hall.

LXXIII: I am describing here a photograph of a silvan scene taken by Frank Meadow Sutcliffe (1853-1941), and the first draft of the poem was sent to my Beloved with a print of that photograph to commemorate our 'dear-held day'.

LXXIV: Although a much later sonnet — and one of reviving, not diminishing hope — this one is very evocative of No. XXXIX, above.

LXXXVI: This poem, with its reference to Odysseus's return and to Penelope's constancy, marks a further growth in confidence which points upward towards the triumphant finale.

CIII, lns. 13-14: The reference is to my Beloved's compassion and tenderness described in sonnets XXXIII-V, above.

Ballade of the Rainbow: Rollinat's poem, which I discovered after writing sonnet CIV, develops so well the rainbow image in association with a many-hued and deeply salutary relationship that I decided to include a translation here. Rollinat has been grossly caricatured as a morbid poet of the decadence; few in fact have described more movingly the healing power of true love and of nature.

Index of First Lines of the Sonnets, etc.

After long banishment of heart from heart	LXX
After the hour when happiness is radiant	after XLVI
An evening bathed in gold, pale Grecian light	I
Are all the travels of Odysseus done?	LXXXVI
Around the unturned corner of our fate	LXXIV
A supple swallow who was wont to flute	LXIV
At love's first coming we were both new-born	VII
Believing most in you, and least in me	XLVII
Be my heart's home, with every door flung wide	LXXXVII
Be thou my friend and of all friends my best	X
Come to my racing heart, and let us rove	XCV
Distance shall not untune the pulse of love	XXI
Drawn tense to breaking on the rack of fate	LII
Echoing with glory still but fallen low	XXX
Fate had bereft me of what most I craved	LXXVII
Gleaming new-minted on our pristine night	XXV
Grant me my Darling with her curls drawn high	XCII
Heroic rose, thus long have you prevailed	LXV
How can I say, when such a harm is done	LVII
How hard it is to keep one's loftiest aim	XVI
I am a dreamer — yes, you have it right	LXXI
I am an aesthete and a lover too	XCIV
I am a pagan of the Grecian strain	XIV
I call to thee across an empty world	LIV
I cannot speak your creed and yet I stand	XIII
I could not love thee more, yet shall love more	XV
I dwelt alone in dreams, and if my dream	II
If, in the cycles of slow time, should rise	LXXVI
If on some distant shore these frail words spill	LXIII
I love the little sounds you make in sleep	CII
I love your being like my mother, Earth	V
I meet you, loved one, though the world unkind	LXXX
In some soft place — you have not told me where	XXVIII
In the first days of heaven-granted grace	XLV
In this loud world where worthless words abound	XL
I strode the lane where we had walked before	LXXII
I thought that I had long since learnt to care	XXXIV
It is astounding: time had ticked us on	LXXXIII
Let me tell you about the envious angels	after XXXVI
Let those drab souls devoid of comely parts	XXIX
Let us hold firm, though dire in its resolve	XLIV
Like a nude Goddess in some soaring dream	XCVIII
Like a parched landscape calling out for rain	XXIII
Love at its birth is like the 'given line'	VIII
Lovers are heroes whom both Gods and men	XLIII
Moderns will mock these lines I turn for you	CV
My lips have scarcely yet begun to pay	XXVII
Nothing will change, although the world has schemed	LIII
Not too many eternities away	LXXV
Now that our hearts in such rich hues combine	CIV
O ache of knowing that I cause you pain	XLVIII
O clash of arms where would be clasp of hands	LI
Oh I have kissed the bronze coins at your breasts	CI
One bed that holds us in a swoon divine	C
One word across the voids of space and time	LXXIX
Our life in miniature: you, lithely poised	IX

O worst of hells, to fail one's most beloved	XLVI
Reality's a slum: I shall not dwell	LVI
Reft of the presence that my heart most craves	XX
Schism of psyche, curse of western man	LVIII
Skies had been barred from me by riftless cloud	LXXVIII
Some blissful day, when glory gilds the air	LXVIII
Street of the Stairs, thou ancient cobbled rise	LXVII
Take me aboard those broad-beamed hips of yours	XCVI
Tell me, do you in torrid moments crave	XCI
The book our love is writing with one pen	XVIII
The greatest loves with sharpest fears must dwell	XI
The measure of your love amazes me	XIX
The mists of distance part and now your smile	XCIII
There is a heroine I wreathe in praise	LXXXIX
There is a place these eyes can hardly see	XXXIX
There is a sanctuary in this fraught world	LXXXV
There is a shrine wherein a figure kneels	L
There was a world of gentleness and calm	IL
The storm had wakened me to solitude	LXIX
The streets are filled with emptiness – your face	LV
The sun sinks angry with a rage I share	after LVI
The sun, the fen, the greenery that springs	after CIV
The tears come easier now, for truth's rare wound	LXXXVIII
This misted landscape with envaulting trees	LXXIII
Though Beatrice by marriage-vows was barred	LXII
Though the day's creaking mill may wear the mind	CIII
Through all that comes, remember one sweet night	LXI
To drink your every tear into my breast	XC
To look into your eyes and know of love	LXXXII
To thank all Gods, to tell all men	IV
To thank you for your heart's abundancy	IC
To wake as those first veils fell from the sky	XXXV
Triumph in life brings triumph to our love	XCVII
We are frail polyps, and our pearly reef	LX
Well, Fate. thou blind and blundering wrecker, hast	LIX
We toast 'the century', and those who hear	CVI
What firmer proof than this be there of love	XXXIII
What shallow strangers were we at the first	VI
When a rare heart draws close to me as yours	XVII
When between you and one your soul adores	XLI
When in black spleen the soul, dejected, ploughs	XLII
When I scan lucent skies or vibrant stars	LXXXIV
When I thee fail in love, it springs from this	XXXVIII
When poor love cannot speak to tell its grief	XXXVII
When we have made of night the calm terrain	XXIV
When you are low, my love, remember this	XXII
When you revealed your faith to be so frail	XII
With heart, with soul, with wit, with will	III
Yes, there is still a heaven: in your eyes	LXXXI
You are my blessing, and I bless your name	XXXI
Your eyes, so dark they pale the deepest night	XXXVI
Your person is my world, my fair demesne	XXXII
Your rapture breathes still at my pillowed ear	XXVI
You shed your petals, rose, while I shed tears	LXVI

FP

The Félibrige Press

is predicated upon the possibility,
to put it no higher, that some of the main
and centrally-guided streams of poetry
could be flowing in unfortunate directions,
and on the certainty that such streams
do not tolerate those flowing other ways,
and that the latter have an equal right
to glitter in the sun
if their waters are pure and clear.